DISCOVER
TORONTO

Darcy Street

Toronto Club

richmond/74

BY THE SAME AUTHOR
Discover Ontario
Sex Stuff
Around Toronto
A Tearful Tour of Toronto's Riviera

John Graves Simcoe

DISCOVER TORONTO

John Richmond's illustrated notebook

Doubleday Canada Limited, Toronto, Ontario
Doubleday & Company, Inc., Garden City, New York

ISBN Number: 0-385-14768-6
Library of Congress Catalog Card Number 76-20387
Copyright © 1976
by John Richmond
Printed and bound in Canada by
The Bryant Press Limited
First Paperback Edition 1978

Contents

FRONT
ENTRANCE

TTC
Conductor
1922

Foreword

At a glance, the reader will know —
that this is neither an exhaustive
study of Toronto's history
nor a complete record of its old buildings.
Those buildings that are illustrated
were chosen in some cases because of
their obscurity and drawn —
as a friend once described my work —
'with pen and ink and tongue in cheek...'
Notes for the text
were selected from reliable sources
so that whatever historic stuff
you read here is mostly true
even though some of the facts
have an unruly appearance.

J.R.R
Claremont, May, 1976

Elizabeth Simcoe arrived in Toronto
at the end of July, 1793.
Governor Simcoe took her that day
to visit the townsite
in an area
bounded by Queen Street
on the north
George Street on the west
Berkeley Street,
on the east,
and the bay shoreline,
which used to be just
south of Front Street

Elizabeth Simcoe

John Simcoe bought several tents
in England from the estate of the late
Captain Cook, and these
became the governor's 'mansion'
in York * until the spring of 1794.
Peter Russell wrote about the Simcoes:
"... you can have no conception
of the misery in which they live..."

* On August 27, 1793, Toronto was renamed York
By then, no houses stood here.

By 1800, York's population was 403.

The King's Printer in Upper Canada wrote, in 1801,
"York is just emerging from the woods
but bids fair to be a flourishing town..."

In 1803 a market place was established
on the site of St. Lawrence Hall.

By 1807 a grammar school appeared
at King and George Streets

and the first service was held at the church
built where St. James Cathedral now stands.

Gibraltar Point, so named by Gov. Simcoe,
is called Hanlan's Point today.

Between 1806 and 1809
a lighthouse was built there

of Queenston stone which was landed
25 feet from the site.

Sand carried by lake currents
from Scarborough Bluffs and deposited

in Toronto Bay
had, by 1854, extended the shoreline
a quarter mile south and nearly a mile west
of the lighthouse.

Gibraltar Point

Richmond /75

At King and Frederick Streets
Mr. Quetton St. George opened
a General Store on the ground floor
of his house in 1809.

That same year, York's theatre-goers
watched an American Strolling Company
perform 'School For Scandal'
in a tavern ballroom.
By the end of the decade
several taverns were flourishing
including Mr. Daniel Tiers' Red Lion Inn
in Yorkville (on Yonge near Bloor)
A book store and subscription library
were also opened in 1810.

Bishop Strachan

The Reverend John Strachan became rector
of St James in 1812 and started
the 'Blue School' in 1813.

The rector

had just performed a marriage ceremony on April 26, 1813, when a signal gun BOOMED.... summoning militiamen from as far away as Markham Township.

Fourteen American warships were anchored off the Scarborough Bluffs!

Panic struck.

Doctor Baldwin bundled up his silverware in his black lawyer's gown and sent it to be hidden in a barn.

All 625 citizens of York were terrified.

Some fled. Early the next morning, the attack came.

Around 8 a.m. six ships entered Toronto Bay, their 50 guns started shelling Fort York and its 700 defenders. An ammunition dump EXPLODED killing 35.

1700 American troops waded ashore.

Five hundred barrels of Fort York's gunpowder BLEW UP as the Americans moved in.

38 were killed, 222 wounded. A big chunk of debris fell on U.S. General Pike, breaking his back. He died that day. The defending forces retreated, leaving 62 dead, 77 wounded. It was over by 2 p.m.

British General Sheaffe marched his surviving troops across the Don River and out of history. Rev. John Strachan and John Beverley Robinson and others confronted the victorious Americans. General Dearborn, in a splendid dress uniform promised that York would NOT BE RAZED OR LOOTED.

The official surrender was signed in a house on Front St., following a victory parade to the tune of "Yankee Doodle Dandy" ♪ On April 28, all public money was handed over.

York County Sheriff John Beikie wrote:

"...Then the business of plundering and burning commenced and did not cease until the evening of the 1st inst..."

Five stores were robbed, 13 homes ransacked, York's only printing press was smashed, the church pillaged.

Ely Playter wrote that the town was: "thronged with Yankees... the Government Building, the Block House... all burned to ashes..."

The Court House, the Governor's residence were also burned. On May 1st all troops returned to their ships, which remained in Toronto Bay until May 6th.

The Stars and Stripes fluttered over York for eleven inglorious days, in all.

Fort York Barracks

richmond/75

A year later, Fort York boasted two new block houses
and five other new buildings within the stockade.
Except for some naval shelling on Aug. 5, 1814,
the Fort was never attacked again.
The 1816 Officers Quarters is the only survivor
among 120 houses in York at that time.

By 1823 there were 209 houses, 27 shops
and the new Bank of Upper Canada (1822) at
Duke and George Streets.
Five years later 2,235 citizens lived here. Larger houses
began to change York from a frontier settlement
into a business-like, dignified town.

Queen Street

By 1834 when York was renamed Toronto and it became a city, its boundaries were Parliament St. on the east, Bathurst on the west and approximately at Dundas St. on the north. The centre of town was at King and Frederick.. Lot Street (Queen) was unopened east of Victoria.

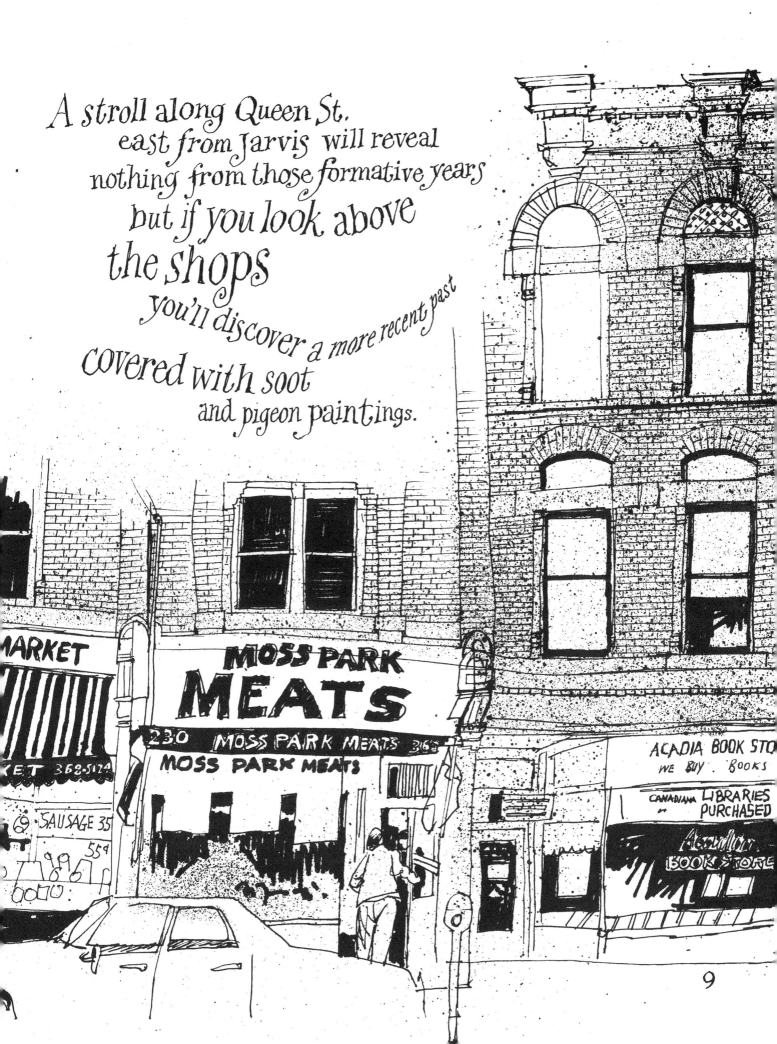

A stroll along Queen St. east from Jarvis will reveal nothing from those formative years but if you look above the shops you'll discover a more recent past covered with soot and pigeon paintings.

MARKET

MOSS PARK MEATS

230 MOSS PARK MEATS 363
MOSS PARK MEATS

ET 368-5124

SAUSAGE 35
55¢

ACADIA BOOK STO
WE BUY BOOKS

CANADIANA LIBRARIES
PURCHASED

BOOK STORE

all have magnificent colored glass sections preserved in grime.

Moss Park had a sidewalk

fé and a Turkish delight candy factory in 1913.

In the 1930's a barbershop like this one would've charged
25 cents for a small boy's haircut.

On the wall, there would've been pinned,
a huge *Old Chum* tobacco poster
with a full color illustration of two
fat, white-wigged English squires
fiddling with long-stemmed clay pipes.

On the south side of Queen at Sherbourne (near Mike's
barber shop) in 1908, the Kaiser Restaurant offered
coffee and donuts for three cents, pie for two cents
and a *blue plate special*: soup, coffee, bread
for a nickel.

Old City Hall / Toronto

nelmond/74

In 1899 when old City Hall opened
the man who signed Toronto's official cheques was also
an artist charged with preparing the
decorative salutations
that were presented to distinguished visitors
such as
Field Marshal Earl Haig
H.R.H. The Prince of Wales
The Right Honourable Lloyd George, etc.
However his elegant, flowing script took a more sober appearance when
signing cheques with his own name, Fred Booz.

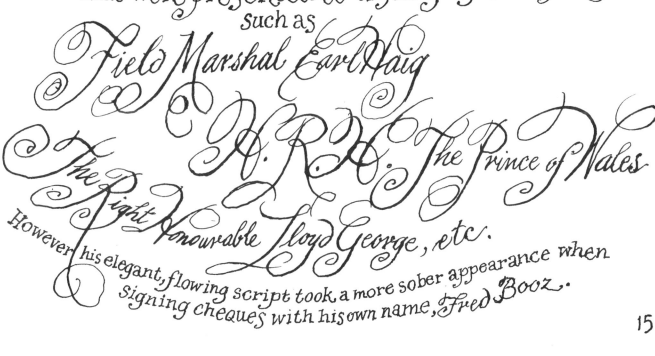

15

The architectural competition for the new city hall challenged its designer to "achieve an atmosphere... that suggests... continuity of democratic traditions..." such as they were.

For example: In 1927 Mayor Thomas Foster suggested that rather than enlarge the police force, the city should simply reimburse any citizen who was robbed.

The next Mayor, Sam McBride, pitched vegetables across the Council Chamber, sometimes raw sometimes canned (the vegetables, not the Mayor).

Almost 30 years passed; then Nathan Phillips, known as "The Old Gray Mayor" called for a new city hall. The new edifice would produce a new era.

Metro chairman Fred Gardiner prescribed the future when during its construction he called the new city hall "An extravagant attempt to build a stairway to the stars."

The many colorful tapestries, ornate murals and precious mosaics that you'd expect to find in a building like this, aren't there, but you can see stars on a clear night.

When Flashing
Garage Full

City Hall, Toronto

17

Sir Wm. Campbell's House, Toronto

At home in its original location on Adelaide St East, Sir William

Campbell (in the 1820's) kept a pet alligator. Toronto's first.

On March 31, 1972, one hundred and fifty
years after it was built,
Sir William Campbell's house was hauled
to its Queen St. site across University Ave.
from Osgoode Hall where Sir Wm. worked
from 1825 until illness forced him
out of his Chief Justice's robes and into
his pyjamas in 1829.
After five years of physical decline, his physician
Dr Henry, prescribed a diet of snipe
which the good doctor rowed across Toronto Bay
to capture for Sir Wm.'s shaky-fingered
dinner.
Dr Henry wrote in his diary:
"On this delicate food the poor old gentleman
was supported for a couple of months;
but then the frost set in...
the snipes flew away
and Sir W. died."

Queen St. West.

Sir John Beverley Robinson became acting Attorney General
of Upper Canada at age 22,
      then Solicitor General at 24, then Attorney General at 27.
   He was elected member of the legislature at 30
      and continued as Attorney General until, in 1830
   he became Chief Justice, Speaker of the Legislative Council
         and President of the Executive Council.
Sir John's portrait hangs over the fireplace in the Great Library
   of Osgoode Hall, where anybody can go and see a picture
   of someone who believed in on-the-job-training.
He also believed, "It is unsafe to trust the government
   to the unskilled and uneducated rabble
      ... those who have to curry favor
            with the vulgar."

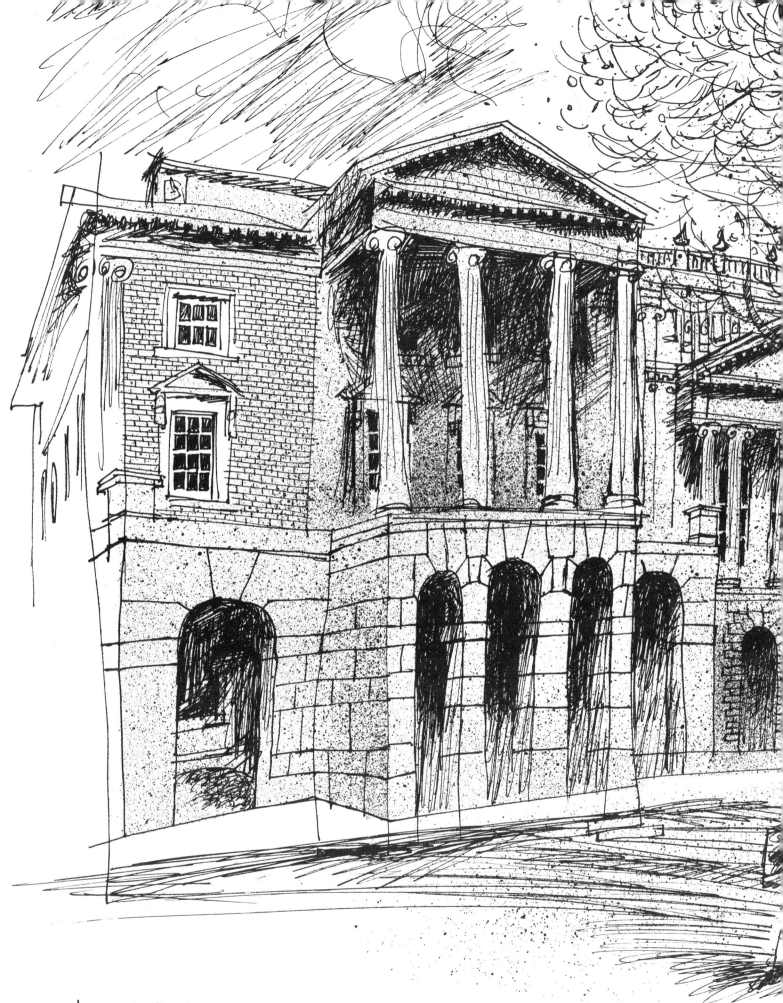

Art students usually take Osgoode Hall too seriously, and won't draw it.

When Sydney Watson showed me this view in 1947, I walked away.   23

Queen Street West, Toronto

24

So certain of their era were these men — architect, builder, stone carver

Jackson
ELECTRIC
APPLIANCE REPAIRS

richmond '74

...nat it was sufficient to mark the decade that Noble Block was built.

About the drawings...

The numerals at the begining of each note indicate the page on which the drawing referred to will be found.

i. The drawing on the title page of Toronto Bag & Burlap Co., on D'Arcy Street, impressed me because it has that no-nonsense bilingual sign.

ii. The Sir Adam Beck monument, at Queen and University, was designed by Emmanuel Hahn who taught at OCA and hosted the first Bohemian party (on Grenville Street) that I ever attended, when I was a small town starry-eyed freshman. There were women at that party who wore long gowns and beads made of stones and I think one or two of them wore green eye shadow. I didn't tell my parents about all that depravity.

iv. The Toronto Club, at 107 Wellington St. West, was started in 1835, making it the second oldest private men's club on the continent, after Philadelphia's. I was in it once as the guest of a pin-striped, horn-rimmed vice president.

3. Gibraltar Point Lighthouse is the oldest surviving structure in Toronto and is haunted. Nobody is allowed inside it unless they're dead *and* ghostly.

7. Fort York's restoration, after over a century of gradual decay, began in 1932. I once met the man who hewed the logs for the barracks.

Fort York is open year round, daily, and a visit there is enlivened by chatty girls in period costumes who make bread and cookies in the officers' kitchen. It's west on Fleet St. from Bathurst.

8. This six-page portrait of Queen Street starts on the north side, at Jarvis. It skips quite a few uninteresting buildings. The original drawing is over five feet long.

14. Mike's Barber Shop and Susanna's Hair Stylist are on the south side of Queen opposite some of the shops in the long picture. I liked the his 'n her contrast in the signs and the plants in Mike's display windows.

15. Old City Hall, seen from the pedestrian bridge over Queen from Phillips Square to the Four Seasons Sheraton. While drawing this, a lady came along and commented that I must be very happy, but I suspect she was being polite and probably meant to say childish.

17. New City Hall is drawn from a perch on the corner of Osgoode Hall fence which lent a feeling of new and old. Notice that parts of the fence are missing.

18. Campbell House, at the corner of University and Queen, has a circular stairway and chimney which runs up the centre of the building with stovepipe openings for all the rooms. Central heating in 1822 was not all that common. The house is open to the public.

21. These stores are along the north side of Queen St., west of Simcoe. This section of Queen has picked up from the days when I was an art student around here. I remember waiting for a bus at Queen and University one night and feeling uneasy about the roary-eyed beverage room patrons who staggered along Queen St. looking for a fight. I was never around when they found one.

22. Osgoode Hall is opposite York Street, on the north side of Queen. Recently restored at a cost of several million, it's a worthwhile place to visit. It was built in three stages, 1829, 1844 and 1857, with this latest work done during 1974 when oak paneling from London's Old Bailey was installed in an anteroom. Originally a boarding school, students paid $40 per year for a bed chamber. I'm not sure how quickly $40 disappears when you're paying court costs nowadays but it certainly wouldn't be measured on a calendar. More likely a stopwatch.

24. Noble Block is on the Historical Buildings List and that's how I discovered it and why I decided to draw it. It's on the north side of Queen, east of Spadina, and is set well back from the road. It's not difficult to imagine a row of Parisian sidewalk bistros along here filled with tourists watching the artists and poets walk by.

27. Whole Earth Natural Food Centre is on McCaul St. just north of Dundas. I was amused by the juxtaposition of this organic grocery store and a Box Lunch where you don't really expect to get crunchy granola.

28. Lawrence Tailoring, on Baldwin Street, is totally unpretentious, and I was told that it's been there for several decades. The fact that it hasn't been all gussied up with vitrolite and a neon sign is what gives it the charm you find only in village neighborhoods like this.

Text continues on page 42

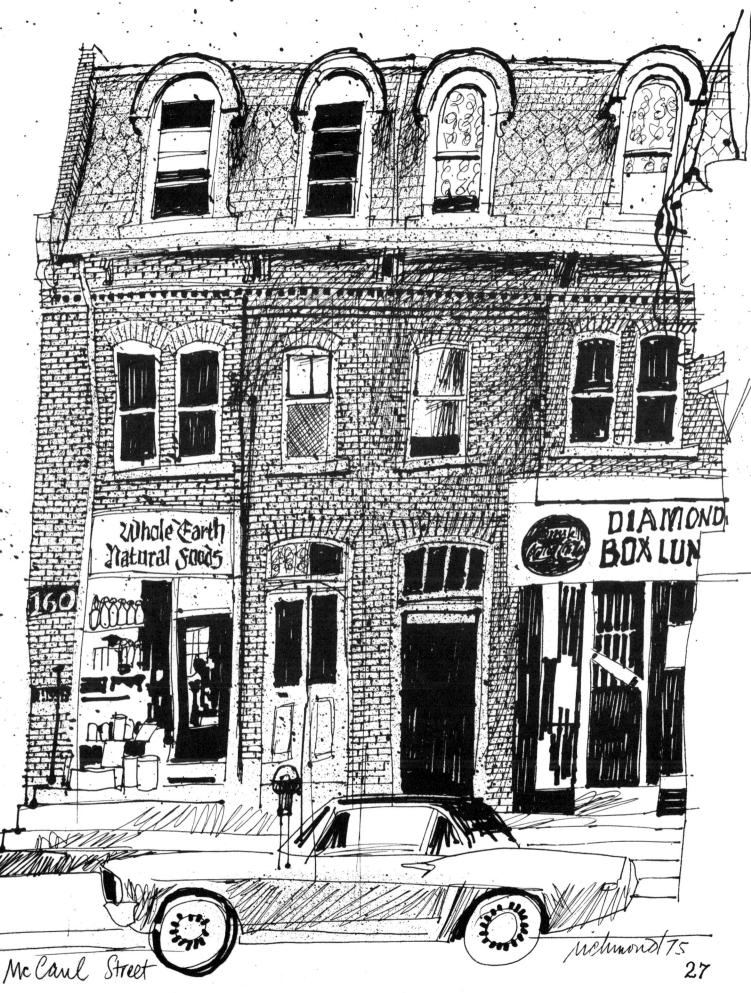

Whole Earth
Natural Foods

160

DIAMOND
BOX LUN

richmond 75

Baldwin St. is named after one of York's superlatively talented, hotshot, busy, elegant, far-sighted*citizens. Wm. Warren Baldwin, doctor, lawyer, architect, town planner, politician, philanthropist, land-owner, laid out Spadina Ave. from Queen to Bloor, then gave it to York.

*see page 5

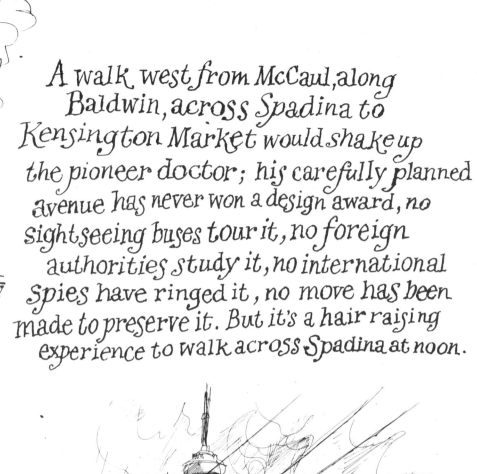

A walk west from McCaul, along Baldwin, across Spadina to Kensington Market would shake up the pioneer doctor; his carefully planned avenue has never won a design award, no sightseeing buses tour it, no foreign authorities study it, no international spies have ringed it, no move has been made to preserve it. But it's a hair raising experience to walk across Spadina at noon.

CN Tower from D'Arcy Street
Richmond/75

29

Kensington

As a student at O.C.A.'s post-war Nassau St campus, I never took those few

venturous steps westward to visit the (then mainly Jewish) Kensington Market

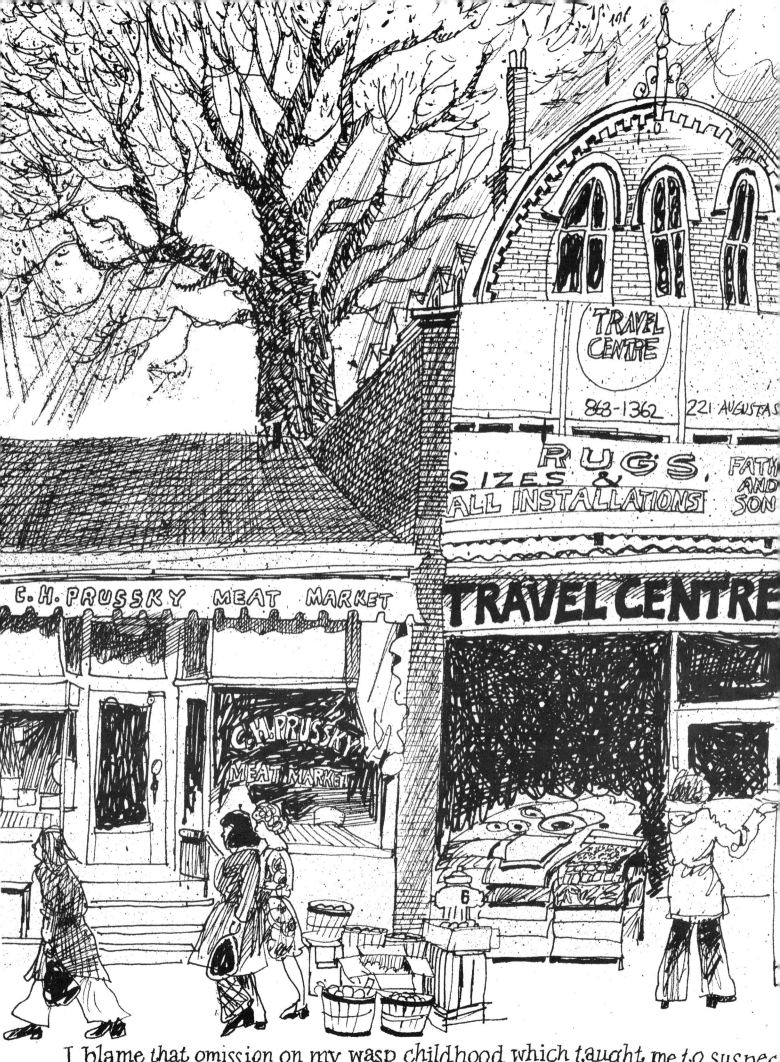

I blame that omission on my wasp childhood which taught me to suspec

...erchandise that wasn't delivered with *respectable British Isles style.*

As anyone will instantly see, these drawings are part reality, part fantas

The reality that I find most fantastic: the Split-down-the-middle houses.

Street theatre happens without stage management. On good days, thousands come

to see the colors and smell the fish and listen to the languages and laughter.

I sat on Beverley Street with my students from O.C.A. one orange afternoon and drew the old Beardmore mansion where, it was said, vast extravaganzas ...complete with glittering guests in horse-drawn Victorias... British royalty dressed in satin braid, tiaras, jewel-encrusted costumes... roast pheasant, imported shrimps, vintage French wines ...footmen, butlers, Upstairs Downstairs maids, maidens... the whole Edwardian glut... happened right here on Beverley St.

Meanwhile, around the corner on D'Arcy St.,. Mr. and Mrs. Alex Eisenberg and their two kids moved into a six-room, two-storey stucco house.

The lot was twelve feet wide by thirty feet deep.

The heating stove cost $1 down and twenty-five cents a week.

Alex brought home $8 from his scrap metal business in a good week.
In 1907 Alex Eisenberg paid $1,200 for his house.

Dundas
& Beverly St.
Toronto 1974

FREE
ENGLISHCLASS
EVERY DAY

richmond

George Beardmore could afford this house because he had neither
wife nor kids to support and his family owned a tannery.

39

The Grange, Toronto

The building shown beside the Grange is my old Art College entrance where

Principal Fred Haines would sit playing a flute until classes began at 9 a.m.

D'Arcy Boulton bought the original Grange property (100 acres) for £300 in 1808 when it reached from Queen St (the town limit of York) up into the wilds of Bloor Street.

By 1875 Goldwin Smith was living in the old (1817) house on the remaining ten acres that were cross-hatched with TALL, mossy fir and elm trees. Cows grazed along Dundas Street at the rear of the property. In 1903 Goldwin Smith wrote, "... what with trolleys, bicycles and automobiles... (driving) is not easy work. Toronto has immensely grown."

30. The Kensington Market in this drawing is, like the drawing of Queen Street, condensed with some shops left out in order to get what I think is the essential look of the market. I stood around here on a squinty-bright afternoon and took snaps then cut out the portions I wanted, pasted them all in a row and made the drawing from that. The market centres around Augusta and Baldwin and operates at its most frantic pitch on Friday and Saturday.

38. The Barber Shop on McCaul St. is at the corner of D'Arcy facing south. I pass this one often on my way north from OCA where I'm currently teaching first year students to experiment with balloons.

39. Chudleigh is a school for immigrants now. They learn how to speak Canadian English which isn't what it was when the house was built at the end of the last century. Back then, English spoken in Toronto was more English than Canadian, just as in Montreal the English was more French, and in Winnipeg more Ukrainian, and so on. Stephen Leacock wrote whole essays on that kind of thing. In Canadian. Chudleigh is at the corner of Beverley and Dundas.

40. The Grange was restored to its 1835 grandeur by Jeanne Minhinnick and Peter Stokes with a little help from some friends. It's south of the Art Gallery of Ontario and is entered from Beverley St. or from Grange Rd. It opens every day, again with costumed girls in attendance, one of whom, below-stairs, offers freshly baked bread and explanations for the Victorian kitchen aids that she has there.

I made a watercolor of The Grange in 1968 and hasti-notes were printed up from that picture which they sell at the door. This version, made after the restoration, shows a more sensitive arrangement of muntins in the circular gable window.

Text continues on page 52

One of the advantages an artist enjoys on the campus of the University is having the space to look at and the elbow room to draw the old buildings.

Another is that college students aren't curious about someone making a drawing the way, say, ten-year-olds are. Young kids will ask to be included in a drawing... "Hey, draw me and my bike!" A college student, likely as not, will detour so as not to walk into your composition.

DO NOT ENTER

University of Toronto.

Richmond/76

This view from Hoskin Ave. looking south across the football field is

University of Toronto   Richmond/75

...e I wanted to draw long ago, but I had to wait 25 years to find out how.

University College, Toronto

This rendering of the south façade of University College was made before its restoration was complete. A long wall of blotchy plywood stood along the length of the building, hiding the famous main entrance, so the base was drawn without foundation planting but without plywood either.

Built in 1856 on part of D'Arcy Boulton's original Park Lot (it's directly north of the Grange), it burned in 1890 and was promptly rebuilt. Among the innovations introduced during the recent restoration was the coating of wooden portions with a fireproof film, the cost of which equalled the Hollywood kind.

47

University of Toronto

When those long curved lines in this drawing came looping easily out of my

en and connected nicely, it was like hearing a clarinet solo, so I kept on doing it.

Richmond/75   49

50

These tall skinny windows and the dome in the old library really grab

University of Toronto.   richmond/76

e. So does that iron mongery deluxe on the U.C. east doorway.

43. Hart House isn't on College St., but in the 1850's when the University of Toronto was built in its present location, as a secular college having no affiliation with the church, it was surrounded by a vast area called College Park. Later this became Queen's Park with an approach from Yonge Street on the east named College Street and from Queen St. on the south (the city limits), called College Avenue, later University Avenue. That the university is now diminished in its territorial domination of the city is a fact that can only be appreciated when the campus is related to the original city after its incorporation in 1834. At the time of the building of King's College in 1842, on the site of the Legislative Buildings (there's a blue plaque on the west side of Queen's Park Cres., just south of Wellesley) the land earmarked for a university was almost a tenth of the total area planned for the entire city.

Dr. John Strachan's campaign to build a university on which Anglican theology would provide a prominent contour was frustrated when University College was chartered in 1857.

University College was to be the core of the apple in this large academic orchard north of the frontier city. But as development took place and Bloor St. became a fashionable address and trees fell under the axe and Taddle Creek was buried and the provincial government moved in at the end of the century with its legislative building where the old insane asylum had been (later during this century more government buildings were added) the campus of the University of Toronto rather than increasing in importance, seems to have worn thinner, like the brow of Jimmy's hill.

54. Central Reference Library, at College and St. George, is slated to face the gallows after September, 1977 when library facilities will be moved to the new Asquith Ave. location. Built in 1905, this chunky old loft was endowed by John Ross Robertson between 1912 and 1919 with over four thousand pictures of historic events in Canada to form one of the largest collections of pictorial history in the country. As an art student, and many times after that, I've spent fascinating hours searching for visual material in the Baldwin Room and the Toronto Room. While the new building will no doubt be more efficient and clever by far, it won't be the quiet wingless flight of imagination that this one was.

56. The Legislative Buildings were fun to draw from this angle. Frank Lloyd Wright called this architectural style "Early Penitentiary," but at least nobody has ever suggested they be torn down, which is something to crow about in almost any modern city.

58. Bloor Street is of course several miles long and this is only a minute section, but I was attracted by the ethnic mix that you find west of Markham St. on the north side of Bloor. As on Queen and in Kensington Market the stores have been compacted to intensify the effect. I would like to continue with Bloor Street across the 'Fifth Avenue' stretch, east to the din-filled Danforth. I grew up here before that war which uprooted many of those who chose to live in Canada and who settled along the Danforth believing that this was a corner of the world where lunatics would be denied access to the knobs and buttons that control whole populations.

Toronto Cop 1915

So far, they've been proven wise in the choice of a place to live, for Danforth bustles peacefully as does all of Bloor St. I hope though, that the garish gleam that has obliterated the original character of the 'Fifth Avenue' stretch doesn't creep too far along this homespun artery.

59. Markham Village is, by some miracle, a commercial blend of artistic insanity and diluted snobbery. It's more fun than Yorkville and would've dried up and blown away years ago except for the Mirvish dynamism whipping up new action at the north end, on Bloor St.

64. Casa Loma is a joke until you try to draw it and then you realize how much it must've cost to build and how prohibitive it would be today and for that reason alone, it's worth keeping. Perched on Wells Hill, looking down over the city, it remains for me a romantic place that as a student I visited for dances. During the fifties and early sixties, artists threw enormous parties there and filled the halls with examples of the best graphic art being done in Canada. Artists' girlfriends wore dresses with plunging backlines, necklines and later climbing hemlines and were braless long before ladies of the revolution shed their underwear. To love this orgiastic mansion you must try climbing the steps from Davenport and walk around from the grounds on the south . . . after dark, in bare feet.

68. Branksome Hall is not so much a handsome building as a backdrop for a handsome fence. Decorum restrains any inclination I might have to describe the rosy-kneed undergraduates pertly skirted in green tartan who can be seen weekdays in the vicinity and who provide reason enough to initiate an exploration of south Rosedale.

70. Craigleigh Gardens, on South Drive east of Glen Rd., was on my way home when I was a twenty-minute-miler. One night, during a spate of reading Joyce's *Ulysses,* I noticed the gate had been left ajar and popped this Joycean corn: "I was sitting in the park when someone left the gate open and I caught a cold." The lady standing at the gates posed with her back to me, but later talked generously about old Rosedale.

71. Perkins Bull House, on Meredith Crescent (to find a path into and out the other side of Rosedale, look at the map on the endpapers of this book), is a well-preserved old pickle which is so stern and furiously earnest that it should be a set for a movie.

Colonel John B. Maclean   richmond/74

Built in the 1870's, it was later bought by Perkins Bull among whose other accomplishments was his facility as a marksman. His grandson grew up and wrote a hostile novel about Rosedale titled *Civic Square* which was published as unbound sheets in a blue Birks gift box. I'm waiting for the movie, now that I've seen the house.

73. The Studio Building is so unattractive to look at, let alone sit and draw, that it's inconceivable for most people to imagine anything exciting ever taking place here. During my session, the lady in the picture walked by, so I asked her to stop and pose. Nobody would sit on the bench, so I made him up. This quite lovely part of Toronto might have inspired a more elegant building if a more sensitive patron had been around at the time. More *sensitive*? Lawren Harris must've been kidding, or was intimidated by the cultural climate of 1913 Toronto and chose to erect this bland pigmentory so as to avoid hostility. Harold Town's personality clashes with the brickwork so I left it out.

74. The Geary House is my idea of a perfect town-house, old, exclusive and hard to find, but only five or ten minutes from downtown.

Text continues on page 76

College & St George Sts.

During the Depression my dad would leave me in the car waiting while he picked

out his weekly library. He read every book they had on Abe Lincoln.

55

56   I visited my brother here one day when he worked in a large office with a

Queen's Park, Toronto
Richmond /75

57

...ine view looking south. It was next to Premier John Robarts' office.

Charles Dickens wrote in the 1840's:

"The town itself is full of life and motion,
bustle, business and improvement.
The streets are well paved
and lighted with gas;
the houses are large and good,
the shops are excellent..."

Hugh Garner wrote in the 1940's
that Toronto "has the best streetcars
and the most stuck-up prostitutes
in the world...
It also has a lot of tough, hard,
sentimental little people...
from Lancashire cotton towns ... the ghettos of Warsaw...
and the narrow alleys of Milan and Budapest."

In 1931 you could rent a ten-room house
at Bloor and Spadina for $50 a month.
Two movie tickets and two dishes of ice cream
after the movie, came to a grand total of 50¢
Prime sirloin beef from prize-winning
Stock at the Royal Winter Fair was
25¢ a pound.

In May, 1831, William Weller, a stagecoach
operator, advertised that :
" MAIL WILL LEAVE YORK SUNDAY, TUESDAY
and THURSDAY at 5 p.m.,
Sleep at Pickering, leave there at 4 a.m.,
breakfast at Darlington,
dinner at Cobourg, arrive at Trenton
in time for steamboats for KINGSTON and PRESCOTT."

61

When I was about twelve years old, I went out to dinner. Nobody else from my family was invited. Although it wasn't on Markham St. it looked like one of these houses (before painted brick caught on) and I was served, among other exotic delicacies, a helping of boiled bat's ears!

They tasted like unsweetened wrapping paper but I ate them, and with chopsticks, since my host and hostess were United Church missionaries just returned from CHINA and their name was (Mr. and Mrs.) Hockey. Really, it was.

MIRVISH VILLAGE

richmond/75

Casa Loma

Casa Loma, Toronto

"Architecturally,
Casa Loma
is a
mixture
of
17th century
Scotch
Baronial
and
20th Century
Fox."

NO
PARKING
ANYTIME

NO
STOPPING

richmond/75

65

Sir Henry Pellatt made money in electricity so he installed 5,000 electric lights in Casa Loma's 98 rooms in 1913, then he invited 1,000 soldiers up for a weekend of bowling and target shooting in his basement. Later, he hosted a dinner dance for 3,000 wealthy Torontonians. When Sir Henry's father said "Henry, sometimes I think you're crazy!" he might've added, 'like a fox,' since Pellatt's grandiose schemes were really real estate promotions that converted a hundred acres (more or less) of raw bush around his castle into the pedigreed privacy that you can peek at today.

Major General Sir Henry Pellatt

I've never been in Branksome Hall
but I once knew girls who went there
so I made this drawing (overleaf)
partly to illustrate Rosedale
and partly to revive old memories
from my college days
when, as the guest of a Branksome graduate,
I supped and sipped with fancy
Toronto scions.

Rosedale, in those days, was a bus route
up until midnight
so that most of my departures
were long, sometimes poetic
pacings south and east
across the Prince Edward viaduct
to where my parents lived
on the other side
of the tracks.

The school is at Elm Ave. and Mt. Pleasant Rd. Before the elm trees

Branksome Hall, Rosedale.

disappeared, it was like walking into an enchanted forest along here.

Craigleigh Gardens, Rosedale

richmond/75

A country house built in 1821 by J. E. Small on 120 acres – bounded on the west by Yonge St., on the east by lower Glen Rd., on the north by Roxborough and approximately at Elm Ave. on the south – was bought in 1824 by William Jarvis whose wife Mary called it Rosedale. By 1875 there were ten houses and by 1900, seventy more. "Rosedale is covered with villas," wrote Goldwin Smith in 1903 and in 1908 he added that the city's social élite "...have fled from crowd, smoke and noise to Rosedale, a happy refuge...with its fine woods..."

By 1905, a map of South Rosedale was printed to assist deliverymen from fashionable downtown shops. Sir Edmund Osler's thirteen-acre estate 'Craigleigh' (1903) was priced at $100,000. in 1924.

Rosedale House

In 1913 Lawren Harris convinced J.E.H. Macdonald, A.Y. Jackson, Arthur Lismer and Tom Thomson to join him in his new studio building in South Rosedale.

Canadian landscape painting was profoundly affected by this alliance when, along with Fred Varley and Frank Carmichael, they formed the Group of Seven. It was 1920 (seven years later, got that?) before they mounted their first exhibition of oil paintings which raised hell with an outraged public. Meanwhile, back at the studio Thoreau MacDonald joined his avant garde father and worked there for twenty-seven years.

He describes his work: "They are all line drawings not because the writer likes this wiry and difficult medium, but because it's cheaper to print than any other. The draftsman can only hope his meaning is clear and try for some of the style and finish we like to see in all good work whether ploughing, carpentry, or a well-built woodpile."

lye

The Studio Bldg. Rosedale

richmond/75

Harold Town now occupies two large
studios there (but not both at the
same time); one of them is adorned
with some of Thoreau MacDonald's

ELEGANT LETTERING, (sigh).

Geary House, Rosedale

On Park Rd. at Meredith Cres., this elegant duchess of a house looks down

the city from behind a tidy fence and a tangle of sidewalk shrubbery.

76. Don Vale is a marvelous little village to walk around and admire the houses, most of which have been given a lot of tender loving care over the past decade. Once, you could buy a cottage on, say, Wellesley St. for $15,000. People I knew did, and they scraped all the paint off doors, baseboards, window frames, everything and found red pine under the fifteen layers of colors. This little store is on Spruce St. and was not busy at all when it should have been, around 5:30 P.M. Hence the For Sale sign. But for voyeurs and passers-by, there's one place you can admire, inside: Pan, 461 Sackville St., which has been a store since 1877 but has been given a transfusion with lots of mod goodies such as Art Nouveau posters and purple soap.

78. The Winchester Hotel is also an interior trip, but I didn't take it since I like the exterior so much, and didn't want to be disillusioned by the color TV or the colorful dialogue that seems almost inevitable in such gingery bars. It's at the corner of Parliament and Winchester where the traffic is still spunky, if not tough.

79. This is a particularly delicate doorway on Spruce Street. From the profusion of pleasing details that you can find in Don Vale, it was more of a task to choose this than I expected. Drawings like this appear in glossy magazines as decorations to relieve the bland look of typesetting and once I submitted a hundred or so to *New Yorker* magazine when I was down there. Such portfolios must pass through that office like luggage at an airport because I got mine back a week later without any indication that it had been examined.

81. Mackenzie House, on Bond Street, two blocks east of Yonge and south of Dundas, is fully restored as a Victorian domestic memento complete with a printing press gallery at the rear of the house where visitors can watch copies of the *Colonial Advocate,* Mackenzie's muckraking paper, rolling off a hand press. One of the most famous legends about Mackenzie tells of when some youthful members of the Family Compact invaded his newspaper office, took his type and dumped it into Lake Ontario. Some versions include his printing press in the dunking. The stunt boomeranged since Mackenzie, who had almost given up on York, sued and won enough compensation to revive his ailing newspaper. This museum is open daily, year round with a special Victorian celebration at Christmas that wows the kids (no matter what age they are).

83. St. Michael's Cathedral manages, in most books about Toronto, to be overlooked even though it's roots are as deep in the city's history as other, more publicized churches. It's biggest drawback is the totally blah grounds, with no approach at all that could be described as suitable for the most important Catholic cathedral in Upper Canada. There are churches in tiny villages in *la belle province* which have more imposing real estate than St. Michael's. In fact, no Catholic church in Toronto has any property to compare with the grounds of say, Metropolitan United Church, just south of St. Michael's. Interestingly enough, Metropolitan's shaded glade is buzzing with nurses and employees from St. Michael's hospital every noon hour but do any of them pop into the church to send up a prayer of thanks for this Methodist calm?

Well, even if there is precious little Catholic shade on a warm Toronto afternoon, there are some pretty spine-tingling notes emanating from young Catholic throats when the St. Michael's boys' choir does its number at mass, particularly around Christmas and Easter. Midnight mass at St. Michael's has to be seen and heard to be believed, since there seems to be lots of room for everybody who can squeeze in the doors. It's an experience not soon forgotten. When I attended my first Christmas mass there, I was seated up in the sanctuary and saw priests dropping bells and fumbling prayer books, all of which gave the impression of watching a football team in a huddle. My harsh opinion of their sanctity was modified after reading Graham Greene and Bruce Marshall who tolerate lapse as reality.

86. Trinity Church was Toronto's first Anglican gate to heaven where no admission was charged. The pews, unlike those at St. James on King Street, were free. For a while, after the disastrous fire of 1849, the haughty establishment was obliged to share this church which was underwritten by an English lady whose identity was a secret for fifty years and whose name I've forgotten.

88. The Yonge Street "Strip" was a difficult drawing to make because it is so deadly dull to walk along there, looking up at all those faded signs behind dusty, vacated windows above the stores. Flotsam notices of bilge business. The visceral arts as gruntingly outlined by raw con artists in day-glo ink with sequin borders amid dark rumblings of the dancing belly.

Text continues on page 90

THE Friendly Corner

FOR SALE
UNITED TRUST

FROZEN FOOD
& FRESH MILK
DAILY

Don Vale, Toronto

Richmond/75

This little store is like one I went to ("mom, can I go to the store"?)
as a kid except there was no frozen food then. Ice cream was
25¢ a brick, soda pop was a nickel, newspapers were
two cents and once a small gang of us emptied
the coin box in a Toronto Daily Star stall
and were chased five blocks by the storekeeper's son
. . . . .dropping all our loot as we ran. . . . .

Parliament Street

richmond/75

From Parliament Street to Riverdale Park
north from Gerrard, in Don Vale
there are Victorian houses built after 1875,
but before then, the General Hospital
was built at Don St.(Gerrard) and Sumach
looking out onto parkland and across
the Don River at the new Gaol.

Don Vale was settled by, among others, a picture framer
(with wife and six children) who earned $8 a week in 1907.
Two boarders contributed $2.50 a week;
the kids ran errands to pay for their boots,
mother got second-hand clothes through charity.

No money was spent on amusements
or holidays except for the Picture Framers'
Annual Eyelet Festival at Hanlan's
Point, otherwise the boys
romped in the lush Don Valley
and skinny-dipped (as I did, 25
years later) in the still sweet river;

the girls lined up to get free
skim milk from the Fred Victor
Mission at Queen and Jarvis.
In 1913 a pound of butter
and a dozen eggs cost
a quarter.

131 Spruce St., Don Vale

79

Bond Street

This drawing of Mackenzie House worked, after many previous attempts to do a satisfactory line drawing had failed.

The others in the book all followed this sketch of the house given to Toronto's first mayor and first rebel leader.

Built in 1850 as one in a row of houses, Wm. Lyon Mackenzie died here in 1861 surrounded by some of his thirteen children and ten thousand memories of his fierce, flaming and futile political career during which he inspired these comments:

"He sat with his feet not reaching the ground, with... the appearance of a madman!" and:

"A multitudinous swarm of lies are buzzing... about him like flies around a horse in August!"

Wm. Lyon Mackenzie

Mackenzie House, Toronto

Back in 1938 before the house at 82 Bond St became
a museum, Prime Minister Mackenzie King
brought two cabinet ministers to see the home where
his famous grandfather had lived.
They stood, with hats-in-hand,
on the sidewalk listening as Mr. King described
its history. In an upper window a curtain moved.
A lacquered finger beckoned seductively.
The bachelor Leader and his two startled colleagues
plopped hats on heads, crumpled into their black
limousine and zoomed dustily away into the sunset.

At the corner of Bond and Shuter Streets, St Michael's Cathedral, 1845, is the
city's oldest church, but it will disappoint those who investigate cathedrals
to find evidence of human mortality which Catholics
take to be self-evident.
Consider instead what Elizabeth Russell wrote at York in 1811:

"The women... are... very prolific. I am acquainted with
a lady that has five pairs of twins... and has buried
several besides. I think it is sixteen she has in all
and is now only about seven and thirty years of age."

I heard variations on that theme uttered 125 years
later, mostly about Catholics or Greeks or Syrians;
any of those uncivilized, insatiable foreigners
but mainly the Catholics.

St. Mike's Cathedral, Toronto

Richmond/74

Yonge Street

Yonge Street was first planned as a highway from Yorkville (at Bloor St.) to Holland Landing in 1794. A road allowance south from Yorkville to Lot St. (Queen) in York was rarely used.

In 1803 Lord Selkirk noted that Yonge St. was well-settled "but no trade passes that way."

In 1808 the Red Lion Inn was built at Bloor after which trade picked up somewhat.

In the 1820's, Dr. Henry Scadding tells us that "the corner of Queen and Yonge was so remote from York that travelers got lost in the woods looking for a house there."

By 1834 there were only a few houses and no shops on downtown Yonge St.

In 1836 Anna Jameson, wife of the Attorney General, wrote, "A little, ill-built town... some government offices built of staring red brick, in the most tasteless, vulgar style... one could be happy here if one could tolerate the flies and frogs in summer and the relentless, iron winter."

By the mid 1860's, over sixty thousand citizens were tolerating Toronto with all its ironies.

Timothy Eaton
1874

84

On December 8, 1869, Timothy Eaton opened his dry goods store on the southwest corner of Yonge and Queen Streets in a three-storey building with twenty-four feet frontage. The purchase price for the property was $6,500. On opening day he employed two clerks and a small boy to wrap parcels. At the door were large baskets of bargains (spools of thread at one cent each) bristling with hand-lettered price cards.

In 1872 Robert Simpson opened his store next to Eaton's. Together, these shops flourished and began to draw trade away from fashionable King St.

Yonge Street became Toronto's 'main drag.'

Within Eaton Centre now under construction (in 1976) will be a relic of the past: Holy Trinity Church (next page), built in 1847. An Anglican rose in a Methodist's mercantile garden.

Eaton's original store on Yonge St. at Queen opened 1869

Within the illustration, the following text appears on the building:

A.D. 184
CHUR
OF THE HOLY TR

86 *My original sketch of Holy Trinity,* *from which this was*

Trinity Square/Toronto

...opied, was made in 1968 when cars, and people without hardhats, abounded.

Across the street from Eaton Centre
along **THE STRIP**
crowds of men and women stroll past
and into a line of peep shows, pop music shops
Salons, saloons and sleepeasies.

ern

Timothy Eat

cin

20

HEAD

SENSUA

NEPTO
HEALT
SPA

STARVIN MARVIN'S | BURLESQUE PALACE

OPEN
9 AM

EXOTIC
DANCERS

STARVIN MARV

STARVIN MARV

EXOTIC GIR
TAKE IT OFF
STRIP REVU

$2.

UNCENSORED
TWO HOURS OF
SEX MOVIES

LADIES OR SENIOR
CITIZENS
also
LOVE AIDS·MAGAZINES
·BOOKS·FILMS·ETC.

COMPLETE
STRIP

331 YONGE STREET

GIVE OR GET A NUDE
BODY RUB
NUDE PHOTOGRAPHY
ALL IN PRIVATE ROOMS

C

Un

MA

$2.00

88

Yonge Street

wouldn't approve such shenanigans. Never. He would've liked the Yonge St Subway though. Looking down on all the dust and burrowing back in 1950 when the subway started, he probably construed that to be the proper execution of his famous advice to study "what goes on at an ant hill."

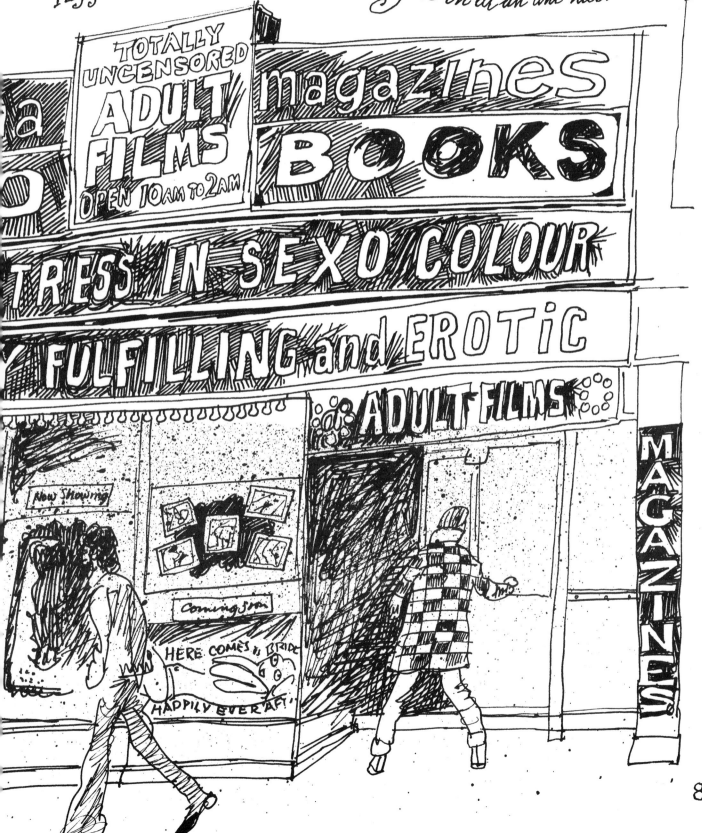

91.   York Belting is for sale for more money than anybody like me can afford. I would dearly love to make studios on the upper floors with that north light filtering through the dust of King St. onto those neat Hollywood windows. When it is sold, I'll be sorry to see the sign disappear. York doesn't get mentioned much in the original part of town.

92.   The Picov Building, at George and King, just a block from the heart of York, was built a long time after the heart had been transplanted over to Queen and Yonge Streets. Mr. Picov is reputed to be a substantial citizen measuring almost seven feet in height. This data is not generally circulated except among very tall or electric people. I like the building and wish there were more of them in Toronto and I hope Mr. Picov stares down on anyone who suggests demolishing the place.

94.   St. Lawrence Hall opened in 1853 and hasn't been going strong since. In fact at one time it was a flophouse. In 1967 it underwent surgery and is now a handsome restoration where you can eat, meet and bleat about anything from politics to polygamy. The Town Hall Restaurant is where you can eat Upper Canadian roast beef priced to meet the rising cost of beefing under the same roof.

97.   St. James Cathedral is across the street from my friend Tom Hodgson's old loft studio. One night I looked out his window at the snow falling around the church. You could feel the muffled hush of the street. It was like a scene from David Copperfield, very muted, almost reverent, and I thought, how penetrating the aura of a cathedral is. You feel it inside your clothes but it doesn't arouse like the touch of living flesh. It's just *there,* around you. Recently I went inside to look at the tablets and the flags and the brasses and the bust of Dr. John Strachan (I spoke to him) and I agree, there's much of this place embedded there. Its Britishness, for sure. It's at the corner of Church and King Streets.

98.   The Royal Alexandra, when I was young, offered orange soda between acts when all other theatres in the world offered hard booze. In 1963, Premier John Robarts and Ed Mirvish changed all that and spiked the drinks with home-grown whiskey that for years had enlivened performances from Rangoon to New Haven. Whether the action on stage has improved or not is of little importance. What matters is that people who get all tooled up for live theatre need lubrication and now they can have it at the Royal Alex, in Edwardian Splendor which is to say, to excess. The Royal Alexandra is just west of Simcoe on King, and can be seen at night from a 707 at 20,000 feet.

100.   King Street from York St. looking east at quitting time. I snapped this and drew it later.

102.   The Bank of Montreal built in 1885, was the second version on this site, it replaced a bank (1845) where the manager lived over the vault. This building pleases because it has sculpture and inside a dome with colored glass like no committee would approve nowadays. I stood under the parapet of O'Keefe Centre and fell madly in love with this old toad while drawing it and spent, not the hour I intended, but more than three hours, circling around the intricate carving that Messrs. Holbrook and Mollington (sculptors) carved into its formidable crust.

104.   The Beardmore Building was sultry and sooty when I first drew it in 1966 but the man who bought that drawing from an exhibit at the O'Keefe Centre impressed upon me the tycoon artist future that lay ahead, if only I could learn to draw bricks, windows and the occasional car, or streetcar. People had always been easy. With luck, I could become another famous Canadian artist like Sam Zimmerman, who earned obscurity as an eliminatist artist the 1930's. Inside the Beardmore is the Hayloft which serves food and has singing waiters whose big number is Happy Birthday to whoever sits down to celebrate there.

106.   The Canary Grill must be saved.

109.   The Diner can go.

110.   Gooderham and Worts have such lovely names, they deserved all their fortune no matter what they did in these frowning grandfather buildings. I like this drawing because it was a real discovery to find this echoing, hollow place with snow and only a car or two.

113.   King and Berkeley, with architect Joan Burt's restoration office block to the north.

114.   Dalton's is an overweight barfly leaning up against your elbow at the bar but not speaking.

118.   Firehall Theatre, on Berkeley at Adelaide, is in the tradition of Toronto showbiz, doing one thing in a place built for something else.

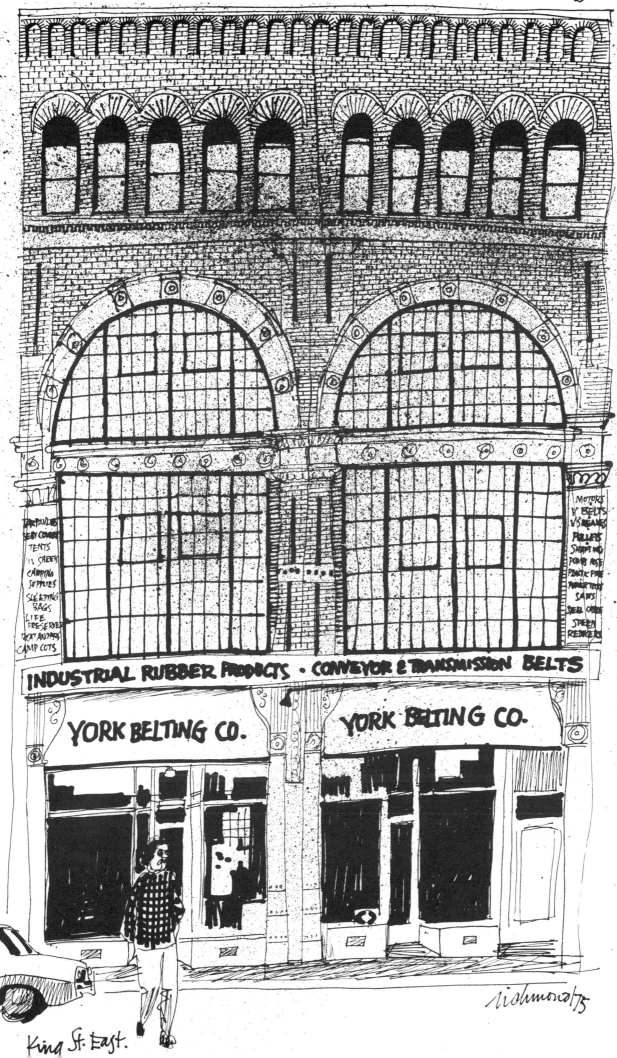

richmond/75

King St. East.

187 King St. East

richmond /75

Most, but not all (see opposite) of our nineteenth-century
buildings have been leveled either by flames
or by demolition crews
so that Toronto achieves architectural balance
only as imagined frames in the cameras
of dreamers like me.
The truth is,
Toronto now has little of its
magnificent past
that can be touched and photographed.

How buildings were built a century ago
sure isn't how we build them now.
While we revere old stuff on TV,
we discard that Victorian, fussy,
time-consuming passion for detailed
whimsy
and we concentrate instead on the lavish use
of mechanically
processed
order.
on architects' renderings, people get smaller
and smaller.

After drawing St. Lawrence Hall
with no visible means of
support on the
east wing,
I read that during
the 1967 restoration,
this part collapsed!

94

richmond /75

95

As you enter St. James Cathedral
you'll see a memorial tablet
on the west wall of the south porch dedicated
to the memory of John Ridout who
died in a duel with Sam Jarvis.
During a row in the street outside his law office,
Ridout whacked Jarvis with a cane across the knuckles.
Young Jarvis then knocked Ridout into the dust.

A challenge from Ridout was accepted
and on a scratchy, stumbling morning
in a clearing in the woods at Grosvenor Ave.
and Yonge St., the two faced each other
with pistols at ten paces.
At the count of TWO! Ridout fired and missed
then apologized, dropped his weapon and asked for another.
The judge eyed him narrowly and ordered Jarvis
to fire at the count of THREE!

On his memorial tablet, Ridout's demise
is described:
"but a blight came and he was consigned
to an early grave on the 12th day of July, 1817
Aged 18."

St. James Cathedral, Toronto

97

richmond/75

Looking at the Royal Alex at noon from this angle is not like seeing it when its several hundred light bulbs flood King St. as though it was a marooned merry-go-round or a back-alley bistro searching the darkness for stragglers.

The Royal Alexandra.
King St. West

richmond/75

PARK

CITY
PARKING

▼

RATES

75¢ EACH HALF HOUR OR LESS

$4.50 DAILY MAX 8am-6pm

$1.00 FLAT RATE AFTER 6 P.M.

$1.00 SAT·SUN· HOLIDAYS

otomat

Canada Ltd

NG AND DEVELOPING

TEPERMAN

King St., Toronto

richmond/75

"The buildings on King Street are grander than those on Yonge; the shops are LARGER and... King Street is honoured by the daily presence of the aristocracy while Yonge Street is given over to the businessman, the middle class and the beggar.

"At three o'clock in the afternoon the first strollers appear. These consist principally of young ladies whose proper place should be at school and young men attired in the height of fashion ... and till six o'clock in the evening one side – for one side only is patronized – King Street is crowded to excess."

—1864 editorial opinion

In 1892, electric street cars inspired the following:

"What will be the result of the trolley's application to King, Queen and Yonge Streets? The trolley will drive carriages off these streets, decrease the value of the property and increase the danger to life ... it is a mistake to accept it . and it will be a curse when it does come."

101

Front Street

Front & Yonge Sts., Toronto

Inside this old toad of a bank, there's a dandy dome skylight. If the Banke

ver tire of it, this would make a heady office space or barber shop.

Front St. East.

104   The man who owns an old drawing of this building (made

efore it was renovated) was afraid publishers would get ink on it.

106

Cherry St at Front St.

This old dowager is hemmed in by scrap yards.

During the 1830's the town of York grew steadily:

"Too many people are crowding into the town
Quenching their thirst at taverns
though they hold no jobs."

At that time the editor of the York Observer wrote:

"We have been in some of the back
townships and have to regret that the scarcity
of hands will occasion the... destruction
of the wheat (crop). Hundred of emigrants...
recently arrived and although unemployed...
they refuse farmers in from the townships
(who offer) 3/9 a day, and board."

From Thomas Magrath's estate 'Erindale', where Hwy 5 crosses
the Credit River, comes this suburban comment
of 1832:

"We have frequently occupied the morning
at work in a potatoe field
and passed the evening most agreeably
in the ball room at York"

Front & George Streets

Front and George Street was once a block away
from Leak's Wharf on the waterfront,
around the corner from York's main intersection
at King and Frederick, and a block east
of the Farmers' Market (it still is).
As a restaurant site, it went unnoticed, but
I drew it because it's a corner
that's had a lot of traffic go past
during the last one hundred and
eighty years.

109

Maybe you nee

me Scottish blood to find this attractive.

richmond/74

That stark, wintry view (previous page) of Gooderham and Worts is from Mill Street, looking east. Begun in 1832 as a flour mill, it became by 1860 the largest distillery in Canada. Among its employees, product loyalty was slavish. Wages were paid on the basis of a worker's stated state of sobriety or collapse: "partly drunk; drunk half a day; sleepy drunk; dead drunk; or drunk as David's sow!"

By 1875 over two million gallons of G&W helped to slake The National Thirst.

Having started the distillery in order to use the 'grain payments' from the flour mill, G&W next got into cattle, then built a railway, then opened a bank. Not bad for a couple of guys who started out with a windmill.

Berkeley Street

Berkeley St. at King E.

richmond/74

In 1861 Anthony Trollope wrote:

"The streets of Toronto are paved with wood... as are those of Montreal and Quebec City but they are kept in better order. I should say the planks are first used in Toronto then sent down the lake to Montreal and when all but rotted out, they are... floated off... to the old French capital."

Just south of this pugnacious pile
at Front and Berkeley, were
York's first Government buildings,
burned by Yankees in 1813.

114

Richmond/75

Daltons 1834 Limited
COCONUT MARASCHINO & GLACE CHERRIES MUSTARD

PLUMBING
PPLIES
G SUPPLIES
WE SELL

Berkeley St.

115

"Pistols for two, coffee for one."

During the Christmas holiday, 1799,
in the woods south of Bloor Street, near
Sherbourne, an unholy, silent tension steadily
mounted as Attorney General John White sat
scratching his goose quill will,
"I should liked to have lived for the sake
of my family
but I hope I am no otherwise afraid to die
than a rational being ignorant of
everything but his own insignificance..."

Mrs. White's brother, Peter Russell (who'd been
Upper Canada's top banana) was pacing the floor.

At Berkeley House on the corner of King and Berkeley,
Major John Small was preparing his challenge:

Pistols at twelve paces at dawn
in Government Park
on Front Street
January 3, 1800

Peter Russell took Mrs. White and the kids to his house Petersfield west of town.
On that hollow morning, a nervous voice croaked, "ONE, TWO, THREE!"
The Attorney General's hand held a gun aimed in terror
at a blur.

116

Major John Small squeezed the trigger and sent a bullet between White's ribs through his kidney and into the tangle of nerves along his spine.

John White toppled clumsily, a leaking costume on a real blood, cold snow, my God! stage.

They carried him in a sled to Petersfield and for thirty-six hours he screamed and groaned. Then mercifully, he died. They wrapped his punctured corpse in a sheet and hauled it back to the farm on Bloor St. and buried it in a shallow grave scraped in his orchard. On January 20, John Small was tried and judged not guilty. He'd defended the honor of Mrs. Small after an insult by the deceased.

Mrs. Small was more severely judged. For many years after, ladies in York would boycott parties to which Mrs. Small was invited and when she was unavoidably encountered, they refused to acknowledge her.

Hon. Peter Russell

richmond 75

Seventy years later, workmen accidentally uncovered John White's bones and these were removed to St. James Cemetery on Parliament Street. This was the first fatal duel in York.

117

FIREHALL THEATRE Nº 70 BERKELEY S.

Richmond/75

118   Ten theatres were opened between 1820 and 1849, some in barns,

ne in a Wesleyan Chapel; another had been a carpenter's shop.

Epilogue

Growing up in the city before the last war meant walking a lot. A ride on the streetcar was a luxury; if you had a bike you were hoi polloi. My older brother's buddy had a coupe with a rumble seat (his father was a coal merchant, unaffected by the Depression). Delivering handbills for my father's appliance stores took me all over the city. I must've walked along hundreds of streets and because it was my dad's business, I kept off the lawns, resisting the urge to shortcut over fences. There weren't any apartments over three storeys, as I remember.

Everyone I knew lived in a house with green grass around it. Our butcher Jimmy Tulloch at the corner of Browning and Broadview knew my mother's handwriting and would fill her order that I handed him when I was seven. Our groceries were delivered in a panel truck; the breadman and milkman teased us and knew all our names. The streets were shared by cars, bikes and horses. Garbagemen's horses, icemen's horses, fish peddlers' horses, ragmen's, Eaton's deliverymen's and in summer, vendors who sold raspberries on "flats" off a wagon—walking along the sidewalk shouting "raspberry ripe, raspberry ripe, three for a quarter (qhaahtah!)"

There seemed always to be an empty lot for playing Vikings or Indians and there was the country school yard at Chester School for serious games of rugby and baseball, played with rules. Next to Prince Edward viaduct hardball was played by big, hard-hitting men. A home run went down the slope into Don Valley and once a man jumped off the viaduct; I was the first spectator out of the bleachers and down the hill to see the dead man in a cement culvert three feet square with his legs sticking out the top. He wore long underwear and his shoes were too big and were tied with rope under the instep.

At twelve, I walked home from the CNE (six miles) because I had no money left, and stopped in Riverdale Park when nature called, only a mile from home. We tobogganed there in winter and skated at Withrow Park—crack the whip, tag—and on the frozen Don River, hockey games lasted all day Saturday. In summer we swung on vines from the trees like Tarzan and dropped into the river between the turds.

Danforth Avenue was our downtown. Diana Sweets started there, operated by our Greek neighbors. There were Syrians (fruit markets) and Irish (funeral home) but mostly our neighbors were English and Scottish except for my mother—she insisted that she was a Canadian. She loathed the British crown and the Pope and anybody who went to any church, for that matter. My mother would talk for maybe an hour to another matron who stood on the sidewalk, thirty feet from our verandah where mother would stand, arms crossed; endless conversations were held over the back fence with people who never entered our house.

My mother was a shiny-floor freak. Newspapers were spread over the waxed hardwood for two weeks after polishing day, and the house echoed with screams from the kitchen ordering us not to walk on yesterday's Toronto *Star*. Soon, all of downtown Toronto will be like that; there won't be any tangle or mess and nowhere to hide or throw up. Every vista that I find comfortable to look at and possible to draw seems to make developers and renovators itchy. Like mother was.

My drawings and paintings were on a display wall for a while in the Toronto Dominion Centre. They were behind glass in the concourse where people could stop and examine the work if they weren't in a hurry. I would go in and change the pictures and one day while doing this at one end of the wall a couple of men stopped further along the display and peered into the work. "Well, he sure as hell can't draw horses," said one. "The buildings aren't too bad, though," said two. "All cockeyed, though," said one. "Hmm, yeah," said two.

I have this daydream where I'm on trial for making shaky buildings. The jury is made up of city planners and architects and engineers, who all have T-squares and set squares and sharp pencils. Their mood is fierce as, one after the other, they ask embarrassing questions about my drawings. Why they aren't straight and true. And why they aren't better than they always are. I have only this flimsy excuse, and no defense counsel to embellish it and give it some credibility: "I don't erase, Your Honor."

Some of the foregoing was read aloud at an Urban Studies Symposium at York University, March, 1975.

Index